George Stephenson

An illustrated life of George Stephenson

1781–1848

Adrian Jarvis

A Shire book

George Stephenson: an engraving from the portrait by John Lucas.

Contents

British Library Cataloguing in Publication Data: Jarvis, Adrian. George Stephenson: an illustrated life of George Stephenson, 1781–1848. – (Lifelines; 45) 1. Stephenson, George, 1781–1848 2. Railroad engineers – Great Britain – Biography I. Title 625.1'0092. ISBN-13: 978 0 7478 0605 9. ISBN-10: 0 7478 0605 5.

ACKNOWLEDGEMENTS
The author acknowledges the extensive and valuable help given to him in the writing of this book by Victoria Haworth, Anne-Marie Knowles (Chesterfield Museum), the Reverend C. J. W. Jackson (Holy Trinity, Chesterfield), Roderick and John Shearer.
    Photographs are acknowledged as follows: Alan Ashurst, page 35; Samantha Ball, page 38; Laura Haworth, pages 7, 34; Holy Trinity Church, Chesterfield, page 33 (bottom two); Cadbury Lamb, pages 5, 19, 26 (bottom), 27, 30, 31 (all), 32 (bottom), 37, 44, 46; National Portrait Gallery, London, front cover; Paul Rees, page 24; Roderick Shearer, pages 21, 33 (top), 39, 43. The illustrations on pages 2, 6, 8, 12 and 32 (top) are from *Illustrated London News*; those on pages 4, 9, 10 (both), 11, 13, 15, 17, 18 (top), 25 and 26 (top) are from Samuel Smiles, *Lives of the Engineers: George and Robert Stephenson*, 1874.

Front cover: *George Stephenson: engraved by T. L. Atkinson after John Lucas. (National Portrait Gallery, London)*

Published in 2006 by Shire Publications Ltd, Cromwell House, Church Street, Princes Risborough, Buckinghamshire HP27 9AA, UK. Website: www.shirebooks.co.uk Copyright © 2006 by Adrian Jarvis. First published 2006. Number 45 in the Lifelines series. ISBN-13: 978 0 7478 0605 9; ISBN-10: 0 7478 0605 5.

Printed in Malta by Gutenberg Press Limited, Gudja Road, Tarxien PLA 19, Malta.

Early career

George Stephenson was one of the most famous engineers of all time and the locomotive *Rocket*, with which he is indelibly associated in the public mind, is probably the most famous single machine. There is virtually no contemporary evidence that he had any significant input to the design of the locomotive, which was the work of his son Robert (the subject of another book in this series). This short account of his life sets out to discover, amid generations of inaccurate history, what George Stephenson did and did not achieve. Its conclusion is that although much of what he is said to have done was in fact done by other people, and although some of the things he really did do himself went badly wrong, he genuinely deserves the title 'Father of the Railways'. It then examines how the accepted story came into being and survived for so long.

He was born in Wylam, a coal-mining village a few miles west of Newcastle upon Tyne, in 1781, a time of rapid change. British

Wylam village, where George Stephenson was born. It was almost entirely dependent on its coal mine, shown here, and an ironworks. Much of the housing was owned by these two main employers as 'tied cottages', and wages were reputedly very low. George's father was a fireman for the pumping engine at the mine.

The house in High Street, Wylam, in which Stephenson was born. In 1948, the centenary of George's death, the North East Coast Institution of Engineers and Shipbuilders organised a fund to purchase the house and present it to the National Trust, which still preserves it. It looks quite spacious, but the Stephenson family occupied only one room of it!

manufacturing, especially the textile industry, was expanding enormously, bringing corresponding expansion in the metalworking trades for machine-building – and in coal-mining for metal production. At Coalbrookdale, Shropshire, the Iron Bridge was recently completed and in once rural Anglesey Thomas Williams, the 'Copper King', was building his business. The Pennine lead and Cornish tin industries were expanding fast. James Watt had built his first rotative steam engine, which was largely symbolic at this date but would soon provide the means to drive machinery not just where there was a good head of

Interior view of the single room occupied by the Stephensons, which looks surprisingly neat and tidy considering its obvious deficiencies in storage space.

water for waterwheels but anywhere that coal could be got at a sensible price. In the English Midlands a fast-spreading network of canals was already making coal much more widely and cheaply available, and a burgeoning coastwise coal trade was competing with it.

One of Thomas Williams's markets was for the copper sheathing that enabled Liverpool slave traders to sail faster than their rivals in the infamous 'middle passage', thereby suffering a lower mortality rate in their human cargo and consolidating their domination of the trade. Liverpool slavers were more than simply efficient and their often substantial profits came home for reinvestment in more and better shipping and docks to serve the industries of the north of England, fetching their raw materials, delivering their finished goods and reducing their costs.

At the time the new-born George uttered his first cry, there was one specially significant problem still waiting to be solved: it was that some major coalfields and mineral-producing areas were situated in terrain that made canal construction somewhere between over-costly and downright impossible, and two such coalfields, the South Wales and the Northumberland and Durham, were potentially the most profitable of all if only they could be better connected with the new areas of demand for coal. It would be nearly half a century before George became involved in work which did not somehow relate to the mining industry of the north-east of England.

We know almost nothing of his childhood, for the obvious reason that he was the son of a 'fireman' of a pit-pumping engine, and such people do not pass down muniments rooms to their heirs. Samuel Smiles, author of the first substantial biography of George, manages a couple of pages, but they were written some seventy years after the event and contain many standard narrative components, suggesting they may be largely fictitious. Furthermore, one needs a sharp eye to notice in the traditional accounts that he had an elder brother, James, two younger brothers, Robert and John, and two sisters, Eleanor and Ann. In terms of home life and childhood pursuits, only 'Nellie' normally features, in a much-repeated tale about George earning the money to pay for a bonnet upon which she had set her heart.

Perhaps young George's first paid employment was indeed minding cattle at 2d per day – that is exactly the sort of thing he would have boasted about in retirement, only a few years before Smiles wrote – and he likely did other agricultural jobs at an early age. He then got a job at the Wylam colliery as a coal-picker before graduating to driving a gin-horse at 8d per day. As the pits went deeper, there was a rapidly growing need for pumping plant to drain them and for men to operate it, and by the age of fifteen George is said to have been a fireman at one shilling a day. Within two years he had become a 'plug-minder', overseeing a steam engine; another two years saw him at the top of that particular tree as a brakesman actually controlling the engine. Now at last he had a little time and money to spare to gain the rudiments of literacy and numeracy, which he had previously lacked. But although all this represented progress, when he married Fanny Henderson in 1802, their matrimonial home was only a single room in a cottage at Willington Quay, a village on the north bank of the Tyne, about

NEWBURN PARISH CHURCH

GEORGE STEPHENSON
1781 - 1848
Enginewright, locomotive pioneer and railway
promoter married Frances Henderson on
28 November 1802 and secondly
Elizabeth Hindmarsh on
29 March 1820 in this church.

CITY OF NEWCASTLE UPON TYNE

The commemorative plaque on Newburn parish church, about 8 miles up-river from Newcastle upon Tyne.

7

A slightly fanciful re-creation, entirely based on Smiles's narrative, of George and Fanny (née Henderson) riding from their wedding to their new home on a borrowed farm horse, with Robert Gray (best man, or 'bridesman' in the usage of the day) and Anne Henderson (bridesmaid) following on another. The date was 28th November 1802.

6 miles downstream of Newcastle. It was here, on 16th October 1803, that his only child, Robert, was born, thereby providing another reason for describing George as 'Father of the Railways'.

The significant move occurred in the winter of 1804–5, when he went as a brakesman to West Moor Colliery, Killingworth, about 6 miles north-east of Newcastle. It was owned by the 'Grand Allies', a group of coal magnates whose favour would carry him far. They temporarily released him to take up a contract to superintend the engine of a spinning mill in Montrose, but while he was away his father was blinded in an accident and left completely dependent on George, who had fortunately accumulated the considerable sum of £28 while in Scotland and was also able to resume work on reasonable pay as a brakesman at Killingworth. By this time he had a good deal of experience

The cottage at Willington Quay, the first marital home, where Fanny gave birth to their only son, Robert, on 16th October 1803. It was here that George was said to have supplemented his income by shovelling ballast and mending clocks and to have become friendly with another young man as ambitious as himself but working in a different field, namely William Fairbairn, a future President of the British Association, major manufacturing engineer and key figure in the development of the new science of strength of materials.

with steam engines and was beginning increasingly to involve himself with maintenance of, and even improvement to, engines. Over quite a short period he progressed from engine-driver to enginewright, and in the process got himself noticed as a useful man by the Grand Allies' engineer, Ralph Dodd.

A partial solution to the transport problems of the South Wales and north-east of England coalfields had evolved over the previous century in the shape of the horse-drawn tramroad. These were proto-railways with initially wooden, later iron, rails on which ran small wagons with iron wheels, used to carry coal from the pithead to the nearest water deep enough for coastal ships. The usual reason canals were unsuitable

West Moor Colliery, Killingworth, one of the more important ones in an area where 'The workings of the coal are of vast extent' – and it is very evidently a much bigger operation than Wylam. Interestingly, though, Wylam had tolerably successful steam locomotives ('Puffing Billy' and 'Wylam Dilly') at work before Killingworth did.

The cottage at Killingworth was not exactly palatial, but with one fairly spacious room and a garret it definitely reflected George's modest ascent of the social ladder. It was not to be a happy home, for less than a year after the family moved in Fanny died shortly after giving birth to a daughter, and the child lived only a few months. It was soon after this that George went to work in Montrose.

was severe gradients, which tramroads could turn to advantage because the coal was going, by definition, downhill towards navigable water. A common arrangement was to send the loaded trains down to the shipping berths by gravity, controlled by a brakesman aboard and with a 'dandy cart' at the back, carrying a couple of horses, which then drew the empty wagons back to the top. It sounds primitive, but it worked quite well – until war broke out again in 1803. For five years Britain did little fighting on land, concentrating instead on funding continental allies and achieving complete naval mastery, but when the Peninsular campaigns began in 1808 the army wanted horses for baggage trains to supply its forces. They may not have got quite every available horse, but they certainly got enough to cause the price of those which remained to rise very considerably. This made it worth spending money on researching alternative power sources, just as Richard Trevithick had done with his 1804 Pen-y-darren locomotive in South Wales, the first steam railway locomotive in the world. John Rennie had been using stationary steam winding engines for spoil-raising when constructing the London Docks. George, not unusually, was in the right place at the right time, though he had several threatening competitors at this stage.

His experience so far had been with stationary condensing beam engines which had subordinated power-to-weight ratio to thermal efficiency and continuous operation and were far too large and ponderous for locomotive purposes, but George knew about Trevithick's relatively

High Pit, Killingworth, whose sinking provided further openings for George's talents.

This 1881 engraving is, like the 'riding home after the wedding' illustration on page 8, based on a snippet from Smiles: 'Few, if any [of his workmates], could lift such weights, throw the hammer and putt the stone so far, or cover so great a space at a standing or a running leap.'

light and powerful high-pressure engines, one of which ran at Gateshead in 1805. George obviously had great self-belief, both in the potential of the product and in his ability to supply it. But what marked him out here, as in so many later projects, was that, among a crowd of aspiring innovators, he was the one who got the backing of the men with the money, in this case Sir Thomas Liddell, principal partner in the Killingworth Colliery, to develop a colliery locomotive. That was a remarkable (though not unique) achievement: a working man who would have earned about the same as Sir Thomas's coachman (if the usual perks of upper servants are taken into account) was entrusted with significant 'research and development' funding. It would turn out to be money well spent.

George's efforts at Killingworth were good rather than brilliant, but his second Killingworth locomotive of 1815 worked well enough to boost his credibility considerably. However, an important digression was about to occur.

The safety lamp

As the pit-owners of north-eastern England dug ever deeper, their problems with gas explosions increased. In 1815 a figurative prize – in the shape of the safer getting of deep coal – was on offer along with a cash prize for the design of an effective safety lamp, producing two contenders almost simultaneously. One was the eminent chemist Sir Humphry Davy, the other the unlettered enginewright George Stephenson. It was this contrast in backgrounds which set the scene for a bitter controversy, for the question of who made the first effective safety lamp became more one of class warfare than of truth. Standing back from the issue, it seems that this was about as near as one can find to a genuine case of simultaneous invention – but the two

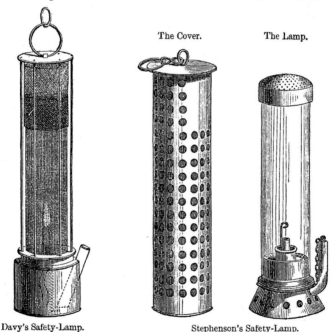

The Cover.   The Lamp.

Davy's Safety-Lamp.   Stephenson's Safety-Lamp.

The Davy lamp and the 'Geordie' lamp. The difference is not obvious at a glance and was obscure to most people at the time of the dispute. Smiles, while clearly favouring Stephenson's claim, pointed out that they were different solutions arrived at in different manners.

13

lamps worked on quite different principles. Reduced to the simplest, the Davy lamp contained the heat of the flame within a wire gauze that dispersed that heat sufficiently rapidly to prevent ignition of gas outside, while the 'Geordie' lamp employed a very small air intake in its base, which made a 'flash-back' virtually impossible. If the worst happened, there was a tiny explosion in the intake which caused an updraught through its chimney sufficient to blow out the flame and prevent ignition of gas outside.

There is evidence that George may have built on ideas of a mining technician named Kit Heppel, and it was Nicholas Wood, Head Viewer at Killingworth, who actually had the prototype made, but it was George who carried out the detail experiments on which all depended and 'packaged' a lamp that worked and was widely adopted in the mines of the region. There really are no grounds for a 'priority controversy' over the Davy lamp. Its more widespread and longer-lasting adoption suggest it was probably the better design, but what mattered was that the lamp controversy allowed George to cast himself as the local champion, downtrodden by the effete scientific patricians of London. The people whose support he sought held exactly similar views: when Davy was awarded the premium for the invention of the safety lamp, local interests raised a testimonial of £1000 for George, who knew he had won. What he had won was not just £1000, but also a fifteen-year Geordie hegemony in railway construction.

The early railway projects

George's first locomotive, though his brother Robert Senior, Robert Junior and Ralph Dodd also had an input, ran at Killingworth in 1814. Robert Senior is an almost forgotten character who participated in a number of George's early schemes. He was Resident Engineer at Hetton (see page 16), was heavily involved in the Bolton & Leigh Railway and was almost solely responsible for the small but difficult Nantlle Railway in North Wales. The Killingworth locomotive had taken most of a year to build. George had visited every working locomotive in the north-east of England, noting their good and bad points, and, as he thought, adopting the good ideas and rejecting the bad ones. His use of straight-cut spur gears to transmit the drive to the wheels apparently

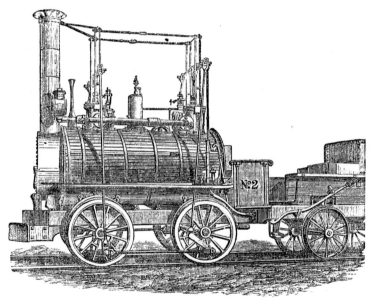

'Old Killingworth Locomotive', 1816. The Killingworth locomotives are confusing, because they were used as testbeds and various key features came and went, including the unsuccessful 'steam springs' – and the blast-pipe, which appears to have been fitted initially at Wood's suggestion but to have been removed by George because it used too much fuel. The benefits of the blast-pipe were much less on a single flue or a return flue than on a multi-tubular boiler. Notice that this locomotive does have outside coupling rods, suggesting an increasing faith in the skills of the men who built it.

led to a good deal of 'snatching', brought about by the inaccuracy of the cast teeth, which were the best that could be managed at the time. In addition, the first locomotive was unsprung and jolted horribly on the rather uneven track, which led, as Smiles put it, to 'considerable derangement to the machinery', presumably a polite way of saying that it shook itself to pieces. But it worked well enough to exhibit great development potential.

Potential was not enough: the first Killingworth locomotive lacked the essential attribute of reliability, a lack which George's 1815 machine set out to supply. Gone were the spur gears: the connecting rods from the overhead crossheads were coupled directly to one axle. According to Smiles, manufacturing problems prevented the use of coupling rods to drive the other axle: be that as it may, chains were initially used for the purpose[1], later being replaced with outside coupling rods. At the same time, George, in partnership with William Losh (patentee of a number of improvements to rails and their chairs), paid attention to the quality of track, for track and locomotive were interdependent in providing reliability. In a third locomotive of 1816 he also experimented unsuccessfully with 'steam springs', which bore the weight of everything except the axles and their bearings, being under the mistaken impression that steel springs could not be made strong enough to take the weight.

Had he looked carefully at the Gold State Coach of 1762, which is still in the Royal Mews today and has a sprung weight of around 2.5 tonnes, he would have seen that the coachbuilders knew how: if they could not make individual spring leaves big enough, they simply used more of them. The steam spring had a short and unhappy existence.

George had correctly identified reliability as the crucial design parameter at this stage and made no attempt at major innovation which might prejudice that. His locomotives, like their competitors, tended to run out of puff under prolonged heavy load, but proved good enough. The steam blast was later added, probably at Robert Junior's suggestion, to the broadly similar locomotives built for Hetton Colliery (1822) and the problem of being a 'shy steamer' was overcome. It was now the way ahead – for a time. Hetton was important for another reason, however: it was the first line for which George was appointed as Engineer – with a capital E. It was also the first for which he was regarded as the leader of a team.

The Stockton & Darlington Railway, initially conceived in 1817,

---

1. The 'quartering' of cranks to allow the use of coupling rods was a difficult task at the time, and one can readily understand a pragmatist like George trying to sidestep the problem.

Edward Pease, the businessman who elevated George from being a fairly successful enginewright to being the Engineer to the first public railway company. He may well have been the one who first thought of using 'Stephenson' as a brand name, creating George's 'rough diamond' image, which served both of them well.

was of a different order of magnitude and involved a private Act of Parliament, which was finally obtained (after much opposition) in 1821. Nicholas Wood facilitated George's contacts, especially with Edward Pease, the leading promoter, and this resulted in his appointment as Engineer. The line as portrayed in the Act in 1821 was simply a colliery tramroad to get coal down from the Bishop Auckland field to deep water. It swiftly evolved into a *public* railway of 40 miles' length (68 km) and a second Act in 1823 allowed both the carriage of passengers and the use of locomotive power. George had persuaded Pease that part at least of the route should be operated by locomotives: a crucial part of that persuasion had been his ability to use the Killingworth line to showcase his locomotive to his most important prospective customer yet. To a risk-taker like Pease the imperfections of the Killingworth locomotives were unimportant: it was the development potential that mattered. This also signified George's belief in railways becoming a national system – he was again looking to the long term, for that same year (1823) he set up the world's first purpose-built locomotive factory (at Forth Street, Newcastle) in partnership with Pease and others, to be managed by his son, Robert. He was determined that he and Robert should dominate the new industry not just of designing but also of

'The No 1 Engine at Darlington'. 'Locomotion No 1' did not exhibit any striking innovations, but she built on strengths and excised weaknesses to become the most practical locomotive so far. The evidence for her being mainly the work of Robert Stephenson and James Kennedy is the account provided by Smiles himself, but published in the United States only, in an edition of 'Lives of the Engineers' by Harper of New York in 1868.

building and equipping railways.

Very little has been written about the process of building the Stockton & Darlington, for the simple reason that little is known. Although the route and gradients were difficult for building a canal, they posed no particular problem when the special constraints of canal construction were removed; indeed, part of the route was surveyed rather like a canal, with

Stockton & Darlington Railway. John Dobbin's sketch of the opening of the Stockton & Darlington Railway in 1825 with 'Locomotion' pulling a train of one coach and some wagons.

The original 'Locomotion' is on show at North Road Station, Darlington.

almost level sections terminated by inclines (the railway equivalent of a flight of locks) where the trains were hauled a short distance by stationary winding engines. The Stockton & Darlington was a considerable success and would serve for later and larger projects as the Killingworth system had for it: it could be demonstrated to potential clients as a system which, although imperfect, really worked.

In 1824, however, George's plans suffered a severe blow when Robert took up a mining engineer's post in Colombia. Initially, the Forth Street Works functioned extremely badly without Robert but, not for the first or the last time, George's talent for finding good assistants allowed him to escape the consequences of his shortcomings in other directions. A young Liverpool man named James Kennedy was brought in and he ultimately ran the works very successfully. As opening day for the S&DR drew nigh, it became clear that there was a problem: no locomotives had been built or even designed, and it was Kennedy who provided the answer. Standing in a corner of the works was a partly completed experimental locomotive named *Active* which Robert had been working on before he left. Kennedy completed it, found that it worked well and then made it a new nameplate: it read *Locomotion No 1*.

This was almost as far as development could proceed without radical changes such as *Rocket*'s multi-tubular boiler, but what evidence there is suggests that at least until Robert's return in 1827, and perhaps later, George was still looking to extrapolate principles first adopted at Killingworth. This is not as stupid as it sounds, for Timothy Hackworth was pursuing exactly that course with some success, notably with his six-coupled monster *Royal Sovereign*.

The Liverpool & Manchester Railway

The Liverpool & Manchester was a 'first' in several crucial ways. It was the first railway to be all steam-hauled, which was important because so long as *any* horse haulage continued (as it long did on the Stockton & Darlington) it was impossible to run locomotives significantly faster than a horse. It was the first to be double-track throughout, which eliminated the unsavoury scenes on the Stockton & Darlington where trains met on single-track sections and the crews argued, and reputedly fought, for precedence. It was the first on which all the motive power belonged to the company: previous railways operated partly on the canal principle of providing a route for other people to use. It was the first to have a signalling system. It was the first to carry mail. It was the first to run to a proper timetable which did not take into account stopping for lunch at some convenient wayside pub in a manner much less organised than that of stage coaches, as was the practice on the S&DR. It was, in short, the first modern railway.

Liverpool's trade had suffered but little from the Napoleonic Wars; indeed in some respects it benefited through being less accessible to French privateers than that of rival ports. The American War of 1812 hit it hard, but only briefly: trade also recovered rapidly from the end-of-the-wars recession and by 1820 at the latest Liverpool was a boom town again. The orthodox story is that there was a problem shipping goods landed in the port to inland customers, with particular reference to cotton and timber bound for Manchester and its immediate environs. This was largely a fabrication: there were three canal routes to Manchester which were of perfectly adequate capacity for the trade and continued to carry most of it (by tonnage) until the 1870s. The old Liverpool–Manchester rivalry came into play to an extent, for the two main canals were controlled from Manchester and the railway would be controlled from Liverpool. But what was really at issue was that this railway was built for a different purpose from any of its predecessors: despite what its promoters said, it was to be a fast passenger line.

The first key figure was a land agent named William James, a man who, acting in his private capacity, saw the nation's destiny as depending on railways. Building on some earlier suggestions, he succeeded sufficiently in enthusing influential merchants and bankers in Liverpool, and especially a leading corn merchant named Joseph

Sandars, that in 1821 he was commissioned to undertake a preliminary survey for the railway. One of his assistants was a promising youth of nineteen named Robert Stephenson. In matters of surveying James was no fool, but his financial judgement was less sound, and problems on other projects found him seriously hindered in his survey work – not least by being three times imprisoned for debt! He struggled to get his affairs in order and deliver the survey but, despite a good deal of tolerance on the part of the promoters, he could not do so, and the work was given to George Stephenson, whose 'interpersonal skills' were about to provide a major pay-off.

Stephenson, as we have seen, had been involved in more successful locomotive railways to date than anyone else, and he had the Stockton & Darlington which prospective investors could visit and travel on. The promoters were aware that much of James's work would be available to George, via Robert and James's son-in-law, Paul Padley, who was quickly snapped up by George. Sandars and his friends had not become as rich as they were by being nice: any notion of respecting James's intellectual property was irrelevant in the context of getting a return on their money. The only contemporary who publicly expressed any sympathy for James's plight was Robert Stephenson himself.

The preliminary survey having indicated that a line was possible at an acceptable cost, the next stage was to produce a detailed survey and estimates in order to obtain an Act of Parliament to authorise the land acquisition, the issue of shares and any necessary borrowing. (One of the strengths of the Liverpool & Manchester was that it did not have to issue any debenture stocks – a form of financing which sank many lesser companies, like Eurotunnel, into bottomless pits of debt.) It is

A pair of surveyor's candlesticks, in the collection of Chesterfield Museum, used for sighting lines and levels in the dark, associated with George Stephenson. The main reason for needing to go surveying in the dark was that there was no legal right to be doing it.

at this stage that we see the roles begin to separate, for George did little of the actual surveying, spending his time instead on the local politics and the fund-raising, where he enjoyed considerable success. The financial climate was dire, a severe cotton 'bubble' following closely on numerous defaults on Latin American government bonds, which caused many failures of Liverpool merchant houses, including some considered very sound. But Sandars was in corn, which was doing well. There is some evidence to suggest that George was not a very good surveyor anyway, but his 'hands-off' approach at this sensitive stage led to a failure of such scale as to jeopardise the whole project – possibly even the whole industry.

When the Bill came before Parliament, the objectors had a strong case and some good lawyers. Some of the pro-railway witnesses, notably John Rastrick, had recent practical experience of major projects and gave cogent evidence for the Bill which the objectors were unable to damage. Stephenson, unfortunately, had not mastered the work his subordinates had done, assuming that he could talk the Bill through in his usual 'rough diamond with a Geordie accent' style, which had served him so well with the likes of Pease and Sandars. This time it did not work: he was faced with an opposing counsel (Edward Alderson) who was able to tear his evidence apart and make it clear that his survey of the railway had been at best perfunctory, more likely downright negligent.

Alderson showed that Stephenson had little or no knowledge of the levels of the track (he could not even prove the location of the datum point, from which everything else was derived) or the likely costs of major structures like the Irwell Viaduct: in the latter case he did not know the width, depth or maximum water level of the river.

This was a poor performance, for an engineer's duties extended to successful promotion of Bills in Parliament, and George was utterly humiliated as Alderson played cat and mouse with him, driving him into a corner, granting him a little respite and then driving him into another. George's ignorance of detail, and his over-dependence on subordinates, were ruthlessly exposed. The Bill fell, and it is astonishing that the engineering career of George Stephenson did not end right there.

But it did not. The time George had spent not surveying he had spent in what would ultimately prove more gainful ways. The promoters did not lose faith either in the railway or in their engineer and went back to Parliament the following year with a somewhat modified scheme produced by George Rennie and his brother John, men whose reputation stood below only that of Thomas Telford. Assisted by Charles

Thomas Telford: detail of an engraving from the portrait by Samuel Lane, 1822.

Vignoles, they refined out the errors and shepherded the Bill through Parliament. George Rennie was subsequently offered the position of consultant engineer, to be assisted by either John Rastrick or George Stephenson. Neither of the latter was a member of the fledgling Institution of Civil Engineers, so Rennie refused and Stephenson was appointed Engineer. Yet again, George had got it right: his friends saw him through.

This was an astonishing achievement: a relatively inexperienced (compared with the Rennies or Telford) and unqualified engineer with the disaster of the 1825 Bill to his name, and with the son on whom he had already been heavily depending away in South America, had 'seen off' two of the stars of the profession and their highly talented protégé. There was more to come, for in 1828 the Exchequer Loan Board Commissioners decided they would check on how their money was being spent on the railway. They consulted Telford, who sent his assistant, James Mills, to make some enquiries. The situation when Telford visited in person the following year was a particularly delicate one. Stephenson had been highly obstructive to James Mills and had been operating a very slack system of works management, on which Mills had made unfavourable comments to his chief. George now needed the approval of Telford himself, because the company needed release of the last tranche of the loan agreed by the Board and without Telford putting in a favourable report they would not get it. The forceful, even bullying, manner George had adopted with Mills melted away, changes were made to the management system, the Loans Board delivered and the Directors were proven right once again in the trust they placed in their engineer – though it may be significant that by this time Robert Stephenson had returned from South America. The directors knew that George was not always very good at the strictly engineering part of the job, but they also knew he was good at finding excellent subordinates and above all that he was a man with the almost monomaniacal vision and ambition needed to see the project through.

Another man with whom George took good care not to fall out was Jesse Hartley, engineer to the Trustees of the Liverpool Docks,

Statue of Henry Booth, by William Tweed, at St George's Hall, Liverpool. Booth was a leading figure in railway development: Secretary and Treasurer of the Liverpool & Manchester Railway, he was responsible for organising the Rainhill Trials and was also a co-proprietor (with George and Robert) of 'Rocket'. A merchant of some standing and a member of a powerful clique of Liverpool Unitarians, he had perhaps a clearer vision of the potential of railways than anyone except William James or George Stephenson.

and Consultant to the Railway, the only person appointed in any potentially competitive role with whom George would hold his counsel. This showed very good judgement: not only was Hartley noted for his short temper and powers of obscene vituperation, he was also the darling of the nonconformist radical group on the Dock Committee[2] – who were well represented on the Board of the Railway Company.

All the preliminary pressure for the railway was geared to the carriage of goods. The canals were represented as slow, inefficient and of insufficient total capacity to handle the trade between Liverpool and Manchester. They reputedly operated a cartel which allowed shameless profiteering. But the membership of the Provisional Committee, and later the Board of Directors of the railway, was made up almost entirely of Liverpool merchants, chiefly in grain, cotton and timber, with a small admixture of bankers. The picture was peddled of Liverpool merchants and Manchester consumers thwarted in their desire to transfer shiploads of grain or cotton to Manchester.

But this was not how the trade worked: Liverpool merchants wished to warehouse goods in Liverpool and sell them on to Manchester when it suited them; that way control rested in Liverpool, which is, of course, why most of the capital for the railway was raised in Liverpool rather than Manchester. The deals were done on the basis of supply and scrutiny of samples and personal bargaining. What Sandars, Cropper, Gladstone, Rathbone and most of the other key figures actually wanted was not a faster way of moving goods but of travelling to and from Manchester (or sending their underlings) to do their deals. It was a matter of moving information and money rather than goods, and that is why the canals continued to carry more cotton than the railway until into the 1870s. It is also the reason why passenger trade – virtually unmentioned (except

2. The Dock Committee was the executive body to which most of the powers of the Trustees of the Liverpool Docks were delegated.

by the discredited William James) before the passage of the 1826 Act – remained more valuable than freight throughout the railway's independent existence. Parliament was deliberately and successfully misled.

Robert Stephenson knew this, and he also knew the answer to the investors' needs: instead of large, slow locomotives of high tractive effort and considerable weight, as favoured by his father, he designed much smaller, lighter and faster locomotives (of which *Lancashire Witch* was the first) which could effect more transport work (in ton/miles per working day) – and also provide a fast passenger service for businessmen. Trust and credit were the essential lubricants of trade, and both would be enhanced by easing the process of doing business in person. That is why the company had a large fleet of passenger carriages available to go into service immediately after opening day – enough to carry two thousand passengers every day in six first-class and four second-class trains each way. Even so, they soon needed more.

But of course George understood that need: he might pose as a working-class hero when it suited, but he had been a part-owner of Willow Bridge Colliery since 1820, so he knew what other businessmen wanted. Once again, his engineering abilities fell short of Robert's, but

'Rocket': probably the world's most famous machine. Like 'Locomotion', she combined all the best of existing practice and shed most of its problems. There is just one question: why was she the only serious locomotive of her generation to have only one driving axle, with quite big wheels, when all the others had either two or three coupled axles and smaller wheels? Could it be to run high-speed passenger trains? The gentlemen who funded the venture said not but perhaps they were not being truthful.

25

The locomotive trial at Rainhill. The most interesting thing about the Rainhill Trials is that the success of 'Rocket' did not result so much from her undoubtedly superior design, as from the fact that all the other contestants broke down. She would have won anyway, but George's passion for things that really worked (to set up the next sale) had been taken up by his son. The difference was that Robert saw high manufacturing standards as allowing both reliability and radical development at the same time.

what he successfully and rightly insisted upon was that there should be no talk of high-speed passenger services until they were proved safe. It is at this point that we must remind ourselves that at the beginning of 1829, when the construction of the railway was far advanced, the form of motive power had yet to be officially determined. It was not until

April that the company decided to hold a trial of locomotives (thus effectively turning its back on horses and stationary engines) and it was October before the famous Rainhill Trials, scene of *Rocket*'s triumph, actually took place.

When the Trials of 1829 made the new high-speed locomotive *Rocket* public knowledge, George himself was at the regulator a fair part of the time. All the evidence suggests that at the age of forty-eight he was quite an impressive figure (sufficiently so to fill the famous actress Fanny Kemble with lust) and in an inspired bit of salesmanship he drove dressed as a gentleman rather than as an engine-driver. Of course it was safe. His laundry bills must have been horrific, but he won the day, a day which shaped the future of the railway industry.

The replica 'Rocket' at the National Railway Museum in York.

Later life and retirement

In biographical terms the Liverpool & Manchester was a hard act to follow, but not because it was an enormously difficult line to build: despite the hype at the time, it posed no civil engineering problems the canal engineers had not beaten decades before. On the locomotive front, *Rocket* was just one of a string of ground-breaking ideas that flowed from Robert's fertile brain. The problem was that the L&MR had been 'first' in so many respects that it almost killed off the pioneer phase at a stroke, because it left relatively little else at which to be first.

But George had always been a rather cautious engineer anyway and it is probably fair to say that the only 'first' which mattered to him after the L&MR was being first to give life to some project or other which was part of his grand vision (or perhaps more properly William James's vision) of a national railway system. In the real world of the 1830s and early 1840s this was no longer simply a matter of engineering skills – and the transition was largely down to George – but also of financial ones, and the two came to intermingle very closely.

One of the first post-L&MR projects with which George was involved

was the Leicester & Swannington Railway, which would make a great deal of money for him, for Robert and for Joseph Sandars, but they did not aim to make it only from the railway: together they bought nearby Snibston Colliery, whose value was enormously increased by the opening of the line to get its coal to market.

During the 1830s there was a minor boom on the railways, which resulted in George being bombarded with offers of large

As with many mining sites, Snibston carried on evolving, to the point where almost nothing very old remains. This is part of the colliery trackbed, now preserved in the Snibston Discovery Park.

sums simply to allow his name, or rather his brand-name, to appear on the company prospectus. He generally and wisely declined such offers unless they were backed by his old and trusted friends of 'The Liverpool Party', a group of L&MR investors who were heavily involved in such blue-chip projects as the Grand Junction (Liverpool–Birmingham) and the London & Birmingham. He was ousted from both, the first by Joseph Locke, the second (which must have been a particularly bitter blow) by Robert. George was irrepressible, however, and went on to work on, among others, the Chester & Crewe, the Chester & Birkenhead and the Manchester & Leeds. This last was a very difficult route, though he capped it by making the first survey for the Chester–Holyhead line, eventually built by Robert and opened throughout in 1848. But there were plenty of other lines for him to work on, including the Birmingham & Derby, Maryport & Carlisle and West Cumberland railways. He played parts of varying importance in many more lines, for some of which he undertook much of the work, through to others like the Ambergate & Manchester where he was a comparatively nominal consultant – though he did have personal interests in Ambergate through his ownership of a massive

Queen Victoria enters a railway carriage attended by George Hudson, 1847. Some biographers have pointed out that there was an element of hypocrisy in the condemnation of Hudson after his fall, because people had been willing enough to accept him when he was rich and famous. Railway promoters did not get much more acceptable than Hudson in this situation.

bank of limekilns which were connected by tramroad with his limestone quarries at Crich and by rail with his colliery at Clay Cross.

Sadly, he did not recognise the railway promoter George Hudson for the crook he was, and allowed himself to be drawn into the York & North Midland Railway and other ventures, perhaps influenced by four testimonials of £2000 each, raised to him by four different Hudson-controlled companies, transactions which caused one author to liken him to Faust. By this time he had added further major coal-mining and limestone-quarrying ventures at Clay Cross to his portfolio – this time in partnership with Hudson rather than his safe old Liverpool friends. But Hudson was one of the greatest white-collar criminals of the century, who did more harm to ordinary thrifty small investors in the space of a year or two than the entire London footpad industry could have achieved in decades. Mr Merdle, the source of so much misery in Dickens's *Little Dorrit*, is based on Hudson.

While the detail of Hudson's method is complicated, the principle is simple. He bought an incomplete or unsuccessful railway which was paying little or nothing in dividends and identified a simple fictitious reason for its failure, such as the need for a connection with another particular line, and went to Parliament to get loan sanction to build the said connection. He then spent much of that (borrowed) money on paying inflated dividends to the *original* shareholders, causing the shares in that company to rise considerably. This convinced the shareholders of the extension line that all that was wrong with their unprofitable venture was the lack of a connection to some other place. An Act was obtained, and now it was their turn to enjoy large dividends paid from the capital of the line to that place. The similarity to the modern 'chain letter' scam is obvious.

The only limit to how many rabbits could come out of Hudson's hat was the credulity of those who put them there in the first place. The Mania was bound to collapse and in 1847 it did, though it did not finally come to an end until 1849. When we learn that George Stephenson rode with George Hudson to purchase the ailing Darlington railway literally for cash from their own pockets we can see how deeply involved he was. The penalty of such transactions was half a million men thrown out of work and even the Bank of England itself imperilled.

There is a damning entry in the diary of the octogenarian Edward Pease suggesting that it was a mercy that George died when he did, implicitly because he was habitually intemperate. But at the time in question probably only elderly Quakers and a few religious extremists cared about such things. It seems likely that Pease was dealing in evasion here: every decent, honest railway investor had both a moral and a financial interest in it not being known how closely George was involved with Hudson. George clearly did enjoy getting drunk on grand occasions, which was quite acceptable at the time and in the circumstances – so long as he retained his integrity in other, more important respects. But he had not, and that, not drink, was why his death was not entirely unwelcome to Pease and other railway investors. The convention of not speaking ill of the dead would serve the railway industry well.

George may seem to have done less during the 1830s than the 1820s, but he still achieved more than many much younger men. Railway construction at this point in history, however, was a very demanding job which took a heavy toll of its practitioners, and by the time he reached the age of fifty-six (in 1837) he was already beginning to think about retirement. But his engineering work had been gradually pushed into the background anyway, as he attended increasingly to the management of his numerous investments in the 'twin firms' and in mining and quarrying. As Hyde Clark, his first biographer, wrote, 'his own property took up most of his time'. He also held a number of offices which demanded some of his time, including the chair of the Norfolk Railway and a seat on the board of the Leicester & Swannington.

His semi-retirement definitely applied only to his engineering and railway promotion work, for in 1838 he leased Tapton House, a small 'stately home' just outside Chesterfield, Derbyshire, to add its extensive

Gaffers Row at Clay Cross was built in 1846 by Stephenson's Clay Cross Company for company foremen.

Tapton House, near Chesterfield, was George's grandest residence. He leased it in 1838 and he retired there in 1843. It was, however, conveniently sited for travelling by rail to the Clay Cross Colliery, the Ambergate lime kilns and the Crich limestone quarries, in all of which he was a partner. The house now serves as a college.

mineral rights to his portfolio. He began a considerable investment programme, again involving some of his old Liverpool friends, in coal-mining, limestone and ironstone quarrying and limeburning. In 1846, while inspecting a route for a proposed railway in northern Spain, he suffered an attack of pleurisy, which convinced him that his engineering days were past, and he retired completely.

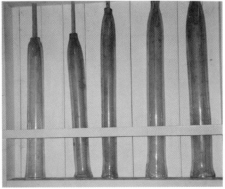

In retirement George Stephenson indulged his love of gardening and he is credited with the invention of the cucumber glass, for making cucumbers grow straight. These are in the Victorian kitchen garden at Normanby Hall, North Lincolnshire.

31

Despite the attacks on George's memory, there was no difficulty in attracting subscribers to a memorial for him. This is the Stephenson Memorial Hall in Chesterfield.

Aside from its mineral rights, Tapton House was (and is) a most attractive house set in beautiful grounds, in which he was at last able to relax to some degree, not just because he could indulge his love of gardening simultaneously with his love of making money, but in the more lasting sense of seeing trains pass through his land, one part of his long-held vision of a national railway system, visible from his sitting room window. When they were laden with coal or lime from his mines, quarries or kilns they looked even better. Tapton House stands on a considerable hill and provided a commanding view, but he did not long enjoy it, for early in August 1848 he suffered a second attack of pleurisy and on 12th August he died.

One can go through the works attributed to George and find that

most of what was good was done by his assistants and, conversely, that some of the things that went wrong were his own work. But that is a naive approach: the chief engineer was captain of a team and the quality of the outcome depended on his successful mixing of different talents in that team. Seen like that, his early works were quite good, but the Liverpool & Manchester – the prototype of the modern railway – was brilliant. A reputation as a great engineer could stand on that alone.

In the end, engineers were no longer people who made things, they were people who got things made. The transition happened almost entirely during George's

The Memorial Hall in its current role as Chesterfield Museum and Art Gallery.

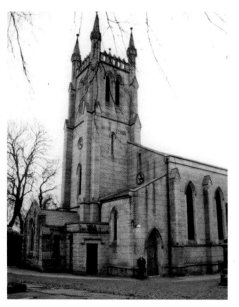

Holy Trinity parish church, Chesterfield, was built in response to a shortage of space in the old church of St Mary and All Saints. The site was donated by the Duke of Devonshire and the foundation stone was laid in 1837. Holy Trinity is still a thriving parish, and the fabric of the church has benefited from major expenditure in the 1990s. It attracts visitors to see the Stephenson memorials (see 'Places to Visit'), who should note that a memorial to George Stevenson outside the church is not the one they seek.

working lifetime: he and his contemporary Jesse Hartley (1780–1860) were among the last great engineers to emerge from the ranks of those who made things to direct skills they did not themselves possess. On those terms George Stephenson was a most remarkable engineer.

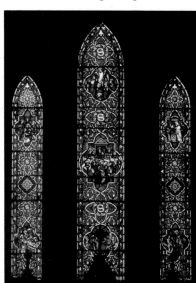

Left: *The east window at Holy Trinity was donated by Robert as a memorial to his father. It bears the monogram GS in three roundels in the centre panel and two in each of the side ones.*

Below: *There is some doubt as to the exact position of George's vault. Partly beneath the north end of the altar table (this is a low church establishment) is this simple incised stone but a little further to the west is a larger memorial slab which appears to cover the vault.*

The biographers go to work

The previous chapters argue that George Stephenson was fundamentally different from the traditional picture of him. Tradition says that he was a brilliant mechanical innovator and a wonderful railway constructor, while history suggests he was not. Tradition claims that he was hindered by being a poor communicator with a rough provincial accent while history suggests that marketing was his strongest suit, despite one major failure when he misjudged his audience. The crucial question in the whole of our knowledge of George Stephenson is this: how could the traditional story be so wrong for so long?

George's death called forth a string of eulogies, notably when John Scott Russell addressed a meeting of the Institution of Mechanical Engineers, of which George had been founding President, and an obituary read by the President of the Institution of Civil Engineers as part of his Presidential Address and published in the *Minutes of Proceedings*.

Such publications were usually generous to the recently deceased, but circumstances dictated that these two would be particularly so: the railway mania had just collapsed and the engineering profession

knew that it would lose a great deal of business and collect a large share of the blame for the ruination of many thousands of small investors. George's death provided a wonderful opportunity for damage limitation. He could become an exemplar of the poor working-class lad made good; the visionary; the genius; the benefactor to all mankind. He could personify intelligence, patience, perseverance and humility in greatness. Above all he could be portrayed as the

Perhaps George's best-known memorial is this statue in Newcastle upon Tyne by John Lough, completed in 1862. The figures at the corners of the pedestal are respectively a miner, a mechanic, an engine-driver and a platelayer.

34

The scene on 28th October 2005, when Stephen Hicklin's fine new statue of George Stephenson was unveiled as the symbolic completion of extensive improvements to Chesterfield station. It is gratifying that the locomotive of which George is holding up a model is not 'Rocket'!

blunt-speaking rough diamond, outdoing John Bull himself in bluff integrity. Because these obituaries were presented in the company of people who had known him well, some of them for a very long time, they were, naturally, believed. Next came a series of articles by Hyde Clark which were bound together to form a little book, and that took the same line.

However, the man who turned George into an engineering hero was Samuel Smiles, whose first attempt at engineering biography, a genre he was to dominate for a century, was a brief life of George in *Eliza Cook's Journal*. Smiles's other claim to fame was his best-selling *Self-help* with its sequels *Character, Thrift* and *Duty*. These strengthened an existing ideological element in the Stephenson story. Self-help was, briefly, a sort of secular religion in which it was possible to rise in fortune, social position and usefulness to one's fellow men by exhibiting exactly those characteristics attributed to George above, all summed up in the expression 'a truly noble and manly character'.

Earlier biographies of famous engineers had not sold well. Smiles had what it took to produce an expensive book that sold out four printings in its first year (1857). He had the support and reminiscences of Robert Stephenson, inside knowledge of railway management, and a job that allowed him to gather oral evidence on Tyneside. Moreover he was an experienced writer. Those were the means: self-help provided the motive.

His *Life of George Stephenson* was a brilliantly written book, whose influence was enormous: as late as 1948, the editor of *The Engineer* lamented the fact that Smiles's success and durability had made it impossible for anyone to publish a more technical and tightly documented work to mark the centenary of George's death. Not until 1960, when L. T. C. Rolt's biography of George and Robert appeared, was there a non-polemic work to reveal that George ever made any mistakes, or to question the key images of 'the rough diamond' and 'humility in greatness'. In May 1990 the Bank of England produced a £5 note bearing a picture of George with three things he did not build: Robert's *Rocket*, Skerne Bridge, designed by Ignatius Bonomi, and *Locomotion No 1*, designed and built by Robert and James Kennedy. Such is the story-telling power of Smiles that eighty-six years after his death he could still persuade the Bank's researchers into believing him.

A cottage industry of authors grew up, writing hack works that invariably peddled the Smilesian line. Sometimes in the quest to show originality they introduced new errors, which other writers repeated.

The uncritical response of academics is surprising but what makes this beatification of George even more remarkable is that there was a small and vocal band who emphatically did not believe that he exhibited a truly noble and manly character. They were all interested parties (which also made them knowledgeable ones), who hounded him beyond the grave. The descendants of William James and Timothy Hackworth were the most vocal, the latter raising their heads at every major railway anniversary down to and including the sesquicentenary of the S&DR in 1975. The universal theme was that George had stolen the credit for the work of their various forebears, which led to disputes over priority of invention.

The knockers were right in that George undoubtedly was a difficult and unscrupulous man, a judgement long spared him by the work of Smiles. Smiles created a myth, in the strict sense of the term – a loose central storyline with certain key ingredients which could become the

This memorial plaque, designed by Amerigo Passani of Florence, is on display at the National Railway Museum, York, and commemorates the centenary of the Stockton & Darlington Railway. It was presented to the British nation by the railwaymen of Italy and shows nicely how the cult of George Stephenson was by no means confined to Great Britain.

subject of variations. Frank Ferneyhough, in his official anniversary history *Liverpool & Manchester Railway 1830–1980*, tells the story of George realising that a skew bridge was needed to carry the Prescot Turnpike (now the A57) over the railway at Rainhill. Not knowing how to do this, the intensely practical man visited the site and stole a turnip from an adjacent field, carved a block model of the bridge with his penknife, and then sliced it up to work out the angles of the stones. This was a waste of a turnip, because Abraham Rees's *Cyclopaedia*, published in parts between 1802 and 1819, had an article by William Chapman on 'Oblique arches', accompanied by some quite nice drawings of them, probably by John Farey.

It appears that Ferneyhough has been misled by Smiles, but his story is not in Smiles. Ferneyhough's telling of it appears to be the earliest written version and he provides no references. He utilised the environment created by Smiles wherein one could tell any story, true, false or indeterminate, provided that it fitted the template of 'Georgeness'. The same can be said of King Arthur or Robin Hood, but there are few figures in recent history of which it is true. Not even Thomas Telford, probably Smiles's second-greatest hero, has made the passage from over-estimation to pure myth.

What was George Stephenson really like?

George Stephenson really did come from a modest working-class background, he was intensely ambitious and he possessed considerable skills in both civil and mechanical engineering, though these were probably of a lower order than has been generally believed. He was a bully, who fawned on magnates like Pease and Sandars but snarled at lesser men. His treatment of Joseph Auty, who was blamed for levelling errors in the first survey of the Liverpool & Manchester Railway, was particularly disgraceful in an age when the chief appropriated the credit for success but took the blame for failure, yet in the main his young assistants succumbed to his charisma. Like Telford, he found it difficult to work with his peers, preferring to be surrounded by admiring and dependent youngsters – and when they got to have ideas of their own, he fell out with them. As mentioned above, just about the only mature engineer with whom he did not fall out was Jesse Hartley, and there were compelling political reasons for that. Although he is portrayed as an engineer, he was also an entrepreneur, through his investments not just in Robert Stephenson & Co and George Stephenson & Son, but in extensive coal, iron and lime production operations.

Such evidence as we have of his life outside engineering (which is largely from Smiles) suggests that he was a completely driven man in his ambitions for himself and, particularly, his son. But hard information on his domestic life is, as with virtually all nineteenth-century engineers, extremely scant. George had three wives, the last of whom he married only in his last year, and of whom we know almost nothing. In *Self-help*

Jesse Hartley (1780–1860) originally trained as a stonemason and then followed his father into bridge construction, eventually becoming Bridgemaster at Salford. In 1824 he was appointed Surveyor to the Trustees of the Liverpool Docks, a post we would now call 'Chief Engineer'. He was an extremely forceful character with a strong belief in integrating engineering work 'in house'. Working for the fastest-growing port in the world, he became the first full-time civilian dock engineer in the world and he was appointed as a consultant to the Liverpool & Manchester Railway.

we find many examples of 'helps meet' – wives of real achievement complementary to those of their husbands. Were Fanny and Elizabeth permanently barefoot and in the kitchen? Figuratively, they probably were, because Robert clearly chose not to tell Smiles anything of consequence about them.

We can identify many faults in George Stephenson, not least that he was probably an objectionable man with whom to do business unless you were in a position of overbearing strength. We can also identify many falsehoods perpetrated and maintained to magnify both his engineering achievements and his personal attributes. To come to a judgement of George's character, we have to decide what we think about ambition verging on monomania. From 1815, when he was only thirty-four years of age, he shared William James's vision that the primitive locomotives with which he was experimenting would become the ruling land transport mode in what was already the greatest industrial economy on earth. He fully intended to be standing there at the regulator, and he succeeded, even if only indirectly. It was Robert, not George, who so revolutionised locomotive design that *Rocket* was obsolete within a year and the *Northumbrian* class which supplanted her was displaced nearly as rapidly by the *Planet* class – and those were just the beginning. But who thought of the idea of the twin firms generating business for each other? Above all, who could recover from the disaster of 1825 to win the business for the younger men? Who else but the Father of the Railways – George Stephenson.

As for the survival of any railwayana dating back to George's day, this plaque on a building near Chesterfield station says it all.

Further reading

Ferneyhough, F. *Liverpool & Manchester Railway 1830–1980*. Robert Hale, 1980.

Jarvis, Adrian. *Samuel Smiles and the Construction of Victorian Values.* Sutton, 1997. Considers material in the text of this work in much greater detail. Fully referenced.

Rolt, L. T. C. *George and Robert Stephenson.* 1960; reprinted Penguin, 1984. The first non-partisan book to challenge Smiles's view of George Stephenson.

Rowland, J. *George Stephenson.* Odham's Books, Watford, 1954. This book is notable for its blow-by-blow account of George's fight with Ned Nelson, the works bully, at Black Callerton – probably fictional.

Skempton, Sir Alec (editor). *Biographical Dictionary of Civil Engineers* (Volume 1, 1500–1830). Thomas Telford Publishing (on behalf of the Institution of Civil Engineers), London, 2002. Useful on Stephenson's contemporaries.

Smiles, Samuel. *Lives of the Engineers: George and Robert Stephenson* (three volumes). Reprinted David & Charles, Newton Abbot, 1968. Numerous other editions available, many showing minor variations. Smiles bestrode the biographical scene for a century.

Smith, Denis (editor). *Perceptions of Great Enginers: Fact and Fantasy.* Science Museum/Newcomen Society/NMGM/University of Liverpool, 1994. A collection of conference papers: see particularly 'Inspiration and Instigation: Four Great Railway Engineers' by Victoria Haworth, 'Samuel Smiles and the Nineteenth Century Novel' by Simon Dentith, and 'The Story of the Story of the Life of George Stephenson' by the present author. Fully referenced.

Smith, Donald J. *Robert Stephenson.* Shire, 1973; reprinted 2003. Companion to this volume.

Thomas, R. H. G. *The Liverpool & Manchester Railway.* Batsford, 1980. The best yet: a wide-ranging, detailed and fairly well-referenced work with much new information. Thorough bibliography for those wanting to dig even deeper.

Young, R. *Timothy Hackworth and the Locomotive.* 1923; reprinted Stockton & Darlington Railway Jubilee Committee, 1975. Perhaps the best example, also giving references to others, of the anti-Stephenson literature mentioned in the text.

Chronological summary

1781	George Stephenson born at Wylam, 9th June
c.1796	Employed as 'fireman' at Wylam Colliery
1798	Promoted 'plug minder'
1800	Promoted 'brakesman'
1801	Brakesman at Black Callerton
1802	Married Frances ('Fanny') Henderson, 28th November
1803	Son, Robert, born at Willington Quay, 16th October
1804	Richard Trevithick's Pen-y-Darren locomotive demonstrated
	Trevithick visits George
	George moves to West Moor Pit, Killingworth
1805	Trevithick's Gateshead loco demonstrated
1806	First wife, Frances, dies
	George goes to work in Montrose
1808	Returns to Killingworth as brakesman; undertakes freelance engine repair work
1812	Appointed as a salaried enginewright by Grand Allies
1814	First locomotive, *Blucher*, ran 25th July (broadly similar to Murray's on Kenton & Coxlodge Railway, 1813)
1815	The safety lamp controversy. Further locomotive experiments
1816	Patent (No. 4067, jointly with William Losh), covering improvements to rails, wheels and the 'steam spring'
	George's last new locomotive for Killingworth
1817	First proposal for Stockton & Darlington Railway
1819	George appointed Engineer to the Hetton Railway
1820	George marries Elizabeth Hindmarsh, 29th March
	George's first independent business speculation, in Willow Bridge Colliery
1821	Goes to Darlington with Nicholas Wood to meet Edward Pease – this leads to his appointment to the S&DR
	First S&DR Act
	Robert (junior) by now playing quite a large part – his name appears on drawings as 'Engineer'
	William James commissioned to conduct preliminary survey of Liverpool & Manchester Railway
1822	Hetton Colliery line opened, 18th November
1823	George a partner in Robert Stephenson & Co (along with Edward Pease, Thomas Richardson, Michael Longridge and Robert)
	Second S&DR Act – authorises locomotive power and passenger carriage

1824	Robert sails for South America, to work for the Colombian Mining Association
	George gains third S&DR Act, secures James Kennedy as works manager of RS&Co
	George Stephenson & Son, the civil engineering arm, founded, with the same partners as RS&Co
	Failure of William James – George takes on most of his projects
1825	Failure of first L&MR Bill
	Passage of Bolton & Leigh Railway Act
1826	Second L&MR Bill passed. George re-appointed as Engineer
1827	George still favours stationary engines for major gradients
	Robert returns, 17th November
1828	Robert visits French engineer Marc Seguin, who has been working on multi-tubular boilers
	Locomotive *Lancashire Witch* (direct-acting, coupled wheels) in service, 1st August: Bolton & Leigh Railway opened
1829	Rainhill Trials, 6th to 14th October: *Rocket* is the only locomotive to complete 'the ordeal' set out in the competition rules
1830	Opening of L&MR, 15th September
1831	Survey of Leicester & Swannington Railway
	Purchase of Snibston Estate
	First survey of London & Birmingham line
1833	Grand Junction Railway Act passed: George joint engineer with Joseph Locke
1834	Joseph Locke appointed sole engineer
1835	Goes to Brussels as a consultant, with Robert: appointed Knight of the Order of Leopold.
1836	Birmingham & Derby line authorised, George as Engineer (opened 1839)
	Set up a London office (9 Duke Street, Westminster) with Robert
1837	Another Parliamentary slip – the London & Brighton Railway
	Replaced by Robert on Birmingham & Derby Railway
1838	Leases Tapton House
	Act for Manchester & Leeds Railway (completed 1840)
	Act for Maryport & Carlisle, completed 1845. Probably the last line George saw through from start to finish
	Second visit to Belgium
1841	Leases Clay Cross Colliery; buys adjoining mineral rights
	Establishes Ambergate lime works
1843	Purchases Tapton House, with mineral rights
1844	Chester & Holyhead Line enabled: George involved but Robert

Chesterfield Museum has a good collection of 'Stephensonalia', including this small panel mounting a snuff box of his, an early Stockton & Darlington Railway ticket signed by him, and some 'season tickets' from the days when these things did not resemble a credit card.

        appointed Engineer

        Third visit to Belgium, to examine route of Sambre & Meuse Railway

1845   Second wife, Elizabeth, dies

1846   Suffers attack of pleurisy while returning from surveying a railway route in northern Spain: virtual retirement from railway work

1847   Institution of Mechanical Engineers founded with George as President

1848   Married again: Smiles relates (in a footnote!) that 'the third Mrs Stephenson had for some time been his housekeeper.' He did not vouchsafe her name (which was Ellen) to history

1848   Second attack of pleurisy: dies 12th August

Places to visit

The number of sites with George Stephenson connections is huge, and he did not go short on memorials either. Many of these places are already indicated in the text or the picture captions, and the ones which follow are simply the present author's favourites, divided into two sections. The first is made up of places associated with George's personal and business life about which there can be no argument, the second to engineering works attributed to him, which the author believes were wholly or mainly the work of others but which were indisputably called into being by George Stephenson.

PLACES DIRECTLY ASSOCIATED WITH GEORGE STEPHENSON

The best day out is to visit Chesterfield and Clay Cross. Chesterfield, perhaps even more than Newcastle upon Tyne, has taken George to its heart. There is much more than just the odd street name or a new housing development called 'Stephenson Court'. Holy Trinity Church (1838) is a must – it even has a small library on George – but it sadly reflects modern society by being locked up when not in use. So you

George Stephenson's statue by Stephen Hicklin stands outside Chesterfield railway station.

have to go there for a service or make an appointment – Holy Trinity Rectory, 31 Newbold Road, Chesterfield S41 7PG. The church is open during the English Heritage 'Heritage Open Days' each autumn.

Chesterfield Museum (St Mary's Gate, Chesterfield S41 7TY; telephone: 01246 345727; website: www.chesterfield.gov.uk) is small but puts up a good showing with a collection of personalia – and the famous Lucas composite painting of the Stephenson family: worth visiting for that alone. The building itself was conceived primarily as a Mechanics' Institute dedicated to George's memory. It is the second-biggest building in the old part of Chesterfield, the biggest being the church of St Mary and All Saints, famous for its crooked spire.

At Chesterfield railway station there is a life-size bronze statue of George by Stephen Hicklin, unveiled in 2005. (Other statues of George may be seen in Newcastle upon Tyne, at the National Railway Museum, York, and in the Great Hall of St George's Hall, Liverpool.)

Tapton House is about five minutes' drive from the museum. The grounds are a public park. The house is a working educational establishment (Chesterfield College/Hallam University) and conducted tours of the interior are few.

The best way to tackle Clay Cross is to get the Clay Cross Heritage Trail leaflet, available in tourist information centres in the area, which includes a number of Stephenson-associated remains.

The site of Snibston Colliery (in production 1833–1983) is preserved by Leicestershire County Council as a 'discovery park', but none of the original buildings survives. (The 'Stephenson Pit' was named to him, not by him.) The section of line from the colliery to Coalville was restored 1998–2001. Further information: Snibston Discovery Park, Ashby Road, Coalville, Leicestershire LE67 3LN; telephone: 01530 278444; website: www.leics.gov.uk/museums

The National Tramway Museum at Crich (near Matlock, Derbyshire DE4 5DP; telephone: 01773 854321; website: www.tramway.co.uk) is housed in a former limestone quarry and parts of the route of the wagonway which ran down to join the main line at Ambergate can still be found.

The Stephenson Birthplace (Wylam, Northumberland NE41 8BP; telephone: 01661 853457; website: www.nationaltrust.org.uk) is maintained by the National Trust and is open on Thursdays, over weekends and on bank holidays. Further information from tourist information centres or the Trust. It is furnished in the style of its social status at the time of George's birth.

Pockerley Waggonway at Beamish, the North of England Open Air Museum. The waggonway dates from 1825 and has an original engine shed of that date. The train shown in this view has the replica 'Elephant' of 1825 drawing two of the characteristic coal chaldrons of the region, together with replicas of contemporary passenger vehicles. While entirely 'repro', this view gives some impression of the state of things at the time of the opening of the Stockton & Darlington Railway.

WORKS ATTRIBUTED TO GEORGE STEPHENSON

The original *Rocket* (with its cylinders lowered as per *Northumbrian* class) survives substantially complete in the Science Museum (Exhibition Road, South Kensington, London SW7 2DD; telephone: 0870 870 4868; website: www.sciencemuseum.org.uk). The National Railway Museum (Leeman Road, York YO26 4XJ; telephone: 01904 621261; www.nrm. org.uk) has two replicas, one sectioned and one working. The original *Locomotion No 1* is still on the platform at Darlington station, and a working replica built 1974–5 normally lives at Beamish, The North of England Open Air Museum (Beamish, County Durham DH9 0RG; telephone: 0191 370 4000; website: www.beamish.org.uk), though it sometimes visits other venues.

It is easy to 'cherry-pick' sites like the remains of the original Liverpool Road Station within the Museum of Science and Industry in Manchester (Liverpool Road, Castlefield, Manchester M3 4FP; telephone: 0161 832 2244; website: www.msim.org.uk), but the experience of standing by the level crossing at SJ 703972 on the Liverpool & Manchester and feeling the ground shake when a train passes gives an idea of what George's team were up against at Chat Moss. The adventurous reader will find

Chat Moss. The difficulties of carrying the Liverpool & Manchester Railway across the 'quaking bog' of Chat Moss were considerable, but exaggerated. James Brindley had succeeded in building the Duke of Bridgewater's Canal over Sale Moor, begun in 1766. More to the point, William Stannard, the contractor for that section of line, had previously built a light waggonway on Chat Moss while he was working as steward to William Roscoe, and so he knew how to 'float' the trackbed.

places like that just by looking at Ordnance Survey maps. It is easy to spot where the engineering problems were – crossings of steep river valleys, running parallel with rivers or canals in narrow valleys and so on. Place names involving 'moss' or 'delph' are a give-away as well.

Do remember that railways are dangerous places and that trespassers may face legal action. Caution is the order of the day, especially if, like William Huskisson, who was killed by a train at the opening of the Liverpool & Manchester Railway, your hearing and your agility are not quite what they once were.

Index

Page numbers in italic refer to illustrations or their captions.